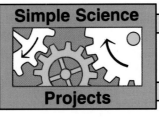

Simple Science

Projects

PROJECTS WITH

FLIGHT

By
John Williams

Illustrated by
Malcolm S. Walker

17986

Gareth Stevens Children's Books
MILWAUKEE

For a free color catalog describing Gareth Stevens' list of high-quality children's books, call 1-800-341-3569 (USA) or 1-800-461-9120 (Canada).

Titles in the Simple Science Projects series:

Simple Science Projects with Air
Simple Science Projects with Color and Light
Simple Science Projects with Electricity
Simple Science Projects with Flight
Simple Science Projects with Machines
Simple Science Projects with Time
Simple Science Projects with Water
Simple Science Projects with Wheels

Library of Congress Cataloging-in-Publication Data

Williams, John.
    Projects with flight / John Williams : illustrated by Malcolm S. Walker.
        p.   cm. -- (Simple science projects)
    Rev. ed. of: Flight. 1990.
    Includes bibliographical references and index.
    Summary: Introduces the concepts of flight through a variety of projects and experiments.
    ISBN 0-8368-0768-5
    1. Flight--Juvenile literature. 2. Flight--Experiments--Juvenile literature. [1. Flight--Experiments. 2.
Experiments.] I. Walker, Malcolm S., ill. II. Williams, John. Flight. III. Title. IV. Series: Williams, John.
Simple science projects.
TL547.W84 1992
629.13'0078--dc20   91-50546

North American edition first published in 1992 by

Gareth Stevens Children's Books
1555 North RiverCenter Drive, Suite 201
Milwaukee, Wisconsin 53212, USA

U.S. edition copyright 1992 by Gareth Stevens, Inc. First published as *Starting Technology — Flight* in the United Kingdom, copyright © 1991 by Wayland (Publishers) Limited. Additional end matter copyright © 1992 by Gareth Stevens, Inc.

Editor (U.K.): Anna Girling
Editor (U.S.): Eileen Foran
Editorial assistant (U.S.): John D. Rateliff
Designer: Kudos Design Services
Cover design: Sharone Burris

Printed in Italy
Bound in the United States of America

1 2 3 4 5 6 7 8 9 97 96 95 94 93 92

CONTENTS

Words printed in **boldface** type appear in the glossary on pages 30-31.

FLYING MACHINES

For thousands of years people have wanted to fly. They looked at birds and wondered how they were able to move through the air.

Today, huge **jets** with hundreds of **passengers** on board travel all around the world. Have you or your friends ever flown in an airplane?

A modern jet like this one can travel thousands of miles without stopping for fuel.

Finding out about flying

The airplane is a fairly modern **invention**. The first airplane that had an engine to power it was flown less than a century ago. It did not look at all like a modern airplane. It was made of wood, cloth, and wire, and its flight lasted only a few seconds.

Before the airplane was invented, people had flown in **hot-air balloons** and **gliders**, but never in a flying machine that had an engine.

1. Research the history of flying. Draw pictures of hot-air balloons, gliders, and the first airplanes. Cut out pictures of different kinds of modern aircraft. Save your drawings and pictures in a scrapbook.

2. Watch the birds near your home. Look at their feathers and the shape of their wings. Draw pictures to show how they move their wings as they fly.

3. Perhaps you have flown in an airplane. Write a story about your adventures at the airport and in the plane.

PAPER AIRPLANES

Making a simple paper airplane

You will need:

A piece of writing paper

Fold the paper along the dotted lines. Carefully follow these drawings, right and below.

1

Fold in half and unfold

2

Fold over

Fold over

3

Fold over

Fold in half

Fold over

4

Fold out

5

Fold up or down

Testing your paper airplane

Throw your paper airplane. Throw it gently, and it will go farther than if you throw it hard.

The flaps at the ends of the wings help steer the airplane. Fold up one flap only and see which way the airplane turns. Now fold one flap down. Does this make any difference? What happens to the airplane when you throw it with one flap up and one flap down?

The Concorde can fly faster than the speed of sound. Look at its shape. Are your paper airplanes a similar shape?

GLIDERS

The paper airplane that you made on page 6 was a very simple glider. Unlike most airplanes, gliders do not have engines to keep them in the air. Once they are **launched**, gliders use their wings to stay in the air and come down gently to the ground.

Gliders are strong and light. Their long, thin wings are specially designed to help them fly long distances.

Making a glider

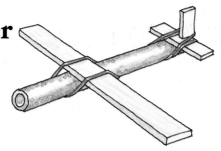

You will need:

*Two pieces of balsa wood, about 3 inches (8 cm) wide and 24 inches (60 cm) long
A junior hacksaw
Foam tubing
Rubber bands
A ruler*

1. For the wings, use a rubber band to attach a piece of wood across the tubing.

2. From the other piece of wood, cut two pieces, one 12 inches (30 cm) long and the other 8 inches (20 cm) long.

3. Measure the edge of the longest pieces and find its central point. At the central point, cut a slot about 3/4 inch (2 cm) into the wood.

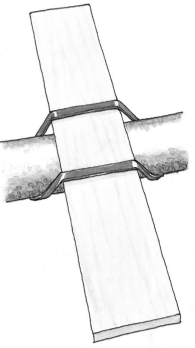

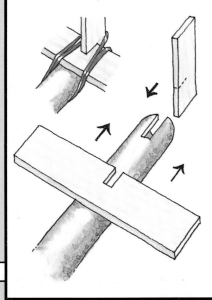

4. Use a rubber band to attach this piece of wood to the tail end of the tubing. The slot should face toward the back.

5. Make another slot 1 inch (3 cm) long in the top of the tubing, at the tail end.

6. Use the shorter piece of wood as the **rudder**. Slide this piece of wood into the slot in the tubing. Attach it to the slot in the other piece of wood and hold it in place with a rubber band.

GOING GLIDING

Flying your glider

Before you fly your glider, make sure it is properly balanced. Prop up your glider by resting the tips of the wings on the backs of two chairs. If the tail end drops, the glider is tail-heavy. To correct this, put some modeling clay on the nose of the glider. If the plane is nose-heavy, put modeling clay on the tail.

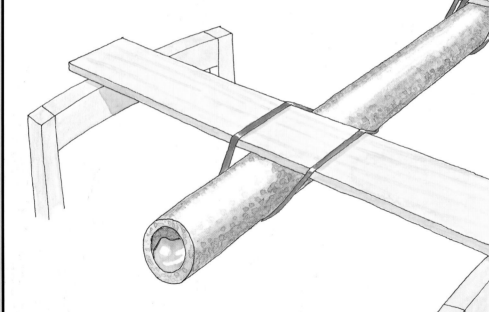

If necessary, slide the wings down the body of the glider. The wings should not be too near the nose.

Now find an open space to try out your glider and see how well it flies.

Further work

Try your glider outside. Does the strength of the wind make a difference to how it flies? Does your glider fly better when it flies with the wind or against it? **Measure** how far it flies on different days.

This is a hang glider. Would you like to try flying it?

HELICOPTERS

When airplanes take off, they must build up speed on a **runway** before they can start flying. Helicopters do not need runways because they can take off straight upward. Helicopters have **rotor blades** on them. When the blades spin around, they lift the helicopter off the ground.

A helicopter has rotor blades instead of wings to keep it in the air. Can you see the blades spinning around?

Making a paper helicopter

You will need:

Cardboard   Tape
Scissors   A ruler
A paper clip

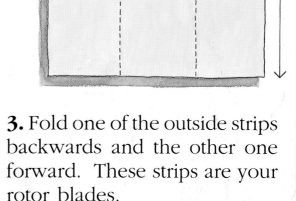

1. Cut out a piece of cardboard that is 3 1/2 inches (9 cm) wide and 5 1/2 inches (14 cm) long.

2. Fold the cardboard into three equal sections. Cut along the creases, leaving about 3/4 inch (2 cm) uncut.

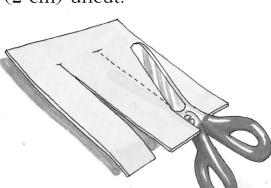

3. Fold one of the outside strips backwards and the other one forward. These strips are your rotor blades.

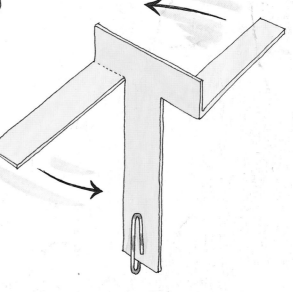

4. Tape the rotor blades to the base of your helicopter to keep them straight out.

5. Attach a paper clip to the bottom of the middle strip of paper, as shown.

6. Hold your helicopter high and let it drop. Watch it spin to the ground.

Making a balsa wood helicopter

You will need:

Two sticks of balsa wood,
   about 5 inches (12 cm) long
Cardboard
Scissors

Glue
A plastic bead
A pin

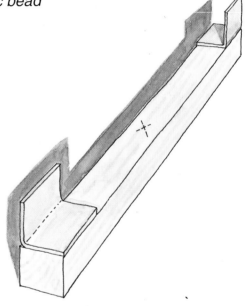

1. Cut out two small pieces of cardboard about 1 inch (3 cm) by 3/4 inch (2 cm).

2. Glue the pieces of cardboard to a stick of balsa wood, one at each end. The cardboard pieces should overlap the wood on opposite sides. Fold up the overlapping cardboard to make flaps. This is your rotor blade.

3. Push the pin through the center of the rotor blade, through the bead, and then into one end of the other balsa wood stick. Make sure the rotor blade can spin freely on the bead.

4. Hold your helicopter in the air and let it drop — just like you did on page 13 with the paper helicopter.

Further work

Try bending the cardboard into different angles on your rotor blade. Does the angle of the rotor blade affect the way it spins?

You can make a pilot for your helicopter. Make a seat out of cardboard. Make a small model pilot from modeling clay and pipe cleaners. Use rubber bands to attach the pilot and the cardboard seat to the bottom of your helicopter. Try your helicopter now.

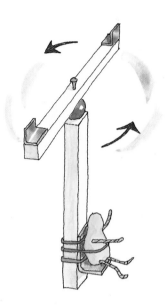

Helicopters do not need runways for taking off or landing. This helicopter is landing on an oil rig far out at sea.

15

 # NATURE'S SPINNERS

Many plants produce seeds, which grow into new plants. When they fall from the plant, they may travel a long way before landing. When the seeds travel, new plants can grow in other places. Some seeds have clever ways of traveling. Some have wings that make them spin around — much like a helicopter's rotor blades. The seeds of sycamore trees are like this.

Look at the wings on these sycamore seeds. Try to find other trees and plants that have seeds that can fly or float through the air.

Experimenting with seeds

You will need:

Sycamore seeds
String
Chalk
A chair

1. Collect as many sycamore seeds as you can.

2. Draw several circles, one inside another, in your school playground or at home on your driveway. To do this, tie some chalk to a piece of string. Get a friend to hold the end of the string on the ground while you draw a circle with the chalk. The **diameter** of each circle should be 3 feet (1 m) larger than the one before.

3. Carefully stand on a chair in the middle of the circles. Drop your seeds one at a time. How far do they fly before they finally reach the ground? Do the seeds fly farther when there is a wind blowing or when it is calm?

4. Test your helicopter in this way. Do the sycamore seeds work better than your paper helicopter?

17

MINIGLIDERS

Leonardo da Vinci was a famous artist and scientist who lived more than 500 years ago. He tried to create a flying machine long before anyone thought it was possible. Since he had no guide other than nature, Leonardo **designed** his model gliders from what he learned about birds.

This seagull is gliding through the air. The shape of its wings helps it fly.

Making a Leonardo da Vinci-style miniglider

You will need:

Plastic straws
Poster board
Scissors
Tape
Modeling clay

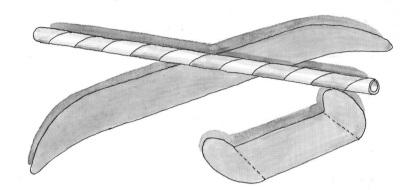

1. Cut out a set of wings and a tail from the poster board. Try to make them look like the shape of a bird's wings and tail.

2. Bend the ends of the wings and tail upward. Tape them onto a straw, as shown.

3. Draw a bird's head on the poster board. Cut it out and attach it to the front of your miniglider.

4. Attach some modeling clay to the front of your glider so that it will balance. Now try flying it.

5. You can make other minigliders the same way. Look around at different birds and copy them to make new designs.

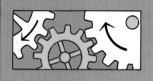
Catapults were used in ancient times as weapons against the enemy. A catapult is a piece of machinery used to fling objects. You can make your own catapult for a paper airplane. You and your friends can test your paper airplanes with the catapult.

This boy is throwing a paper airplane. Do you think his airplane will go as far as the ones you made?

Making a catapult for a paper airplane

You will need:

A short plank of wood   A pencil
Two small nails   A ruler
A small hammer   Scissors
A rubber band   Tape

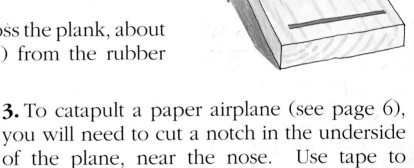

1. Hammer the nails to one end of the plank, as shown. The nails should be about 6 inches (15 cm) apart. Put the rubber band around the nails.

2. Draw a line across the plank, about 16 inches (40 cm) from the rubber band, as shown.

3. To catapult a paper airplane (see page 6), you will need to cut a notch in the underside of the plane, near the nose. Use tape to strengthen the paper around the notch.

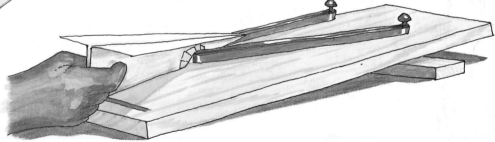

4. Put the rubber band into the notch and pull back the plane until its tail is level with the line you just drew. Let the airplane go and watch it fly.

5. You can use your catapult to test your friends' paper airplanes. Whose airplane flew the farthest? Now try testing your gliders and minigliders with your catapult, too.

WARNING:
Ask an adult to help you use the hammer and nails.

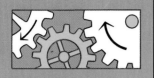

BIRDS

Making a mechanical bird

You will need:

A sheet of thin balsa wood
A junior hacksaw
Glue
A pencil
String
Tape
A wooden stick
Modeling clay

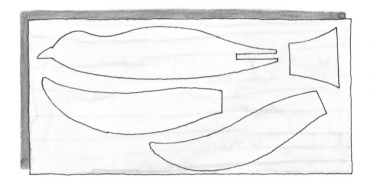

1. On the balsa wood, draw the shape of a bird's body, wings, and tail. Cut out the shapes with the hacksaw. The bird should be about 16 inches (40 cm) long, including the tail. The wings should each be about 8 inches (20 cm) long.

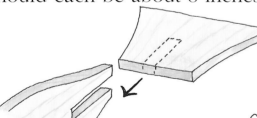

2. Cut a slot in the end of the bird's body. Glue the tail into the slot, as shown.

3. Now tape the wings to the center of the body, about 6 inches (15 cm) from the beak.

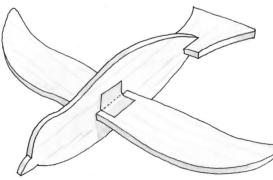

4. Tape a piece of string to the middle of each wing. Tie the strings to the stick. Attach another piece of string to the underside of the bird.

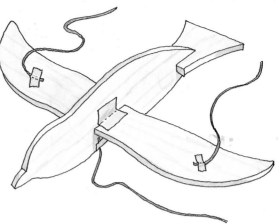

5. To make the bird balance with its wings out, stick small pieces of modeling clay to the head and wing tips, and a larger piece to the string underneath. You will need to experiment with the modeling clay to find the correct amount.

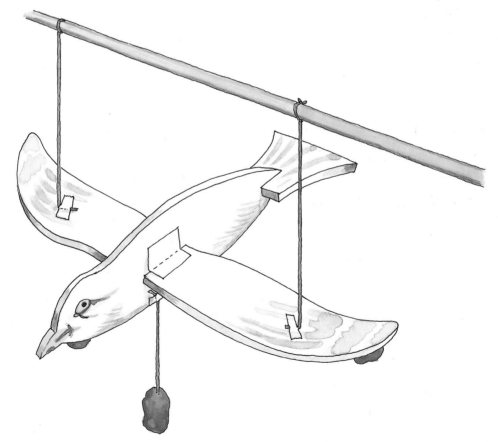

6. When the bird is balanced, gently pull the string underneath and watch the wings flap.

KITES

Have you ever flown a kite in the park or at the beach? Kites can be many different shapes and sizes, but they are all shaped so that the air will lift them up and make them fly.

Making a kite

You will need:

A plastic garbage bag
Two wooden sticks, about
 3 feet (90 cm) long
Masking tape
Scissors
String

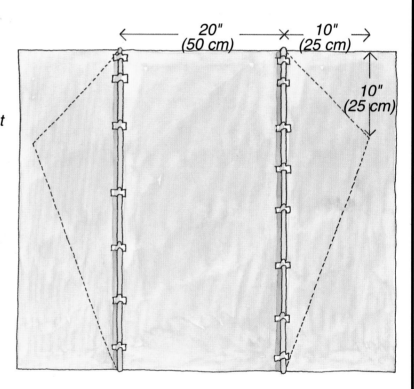

1. Cut open one side and the bottom of the garbage bag. Open it and lay it out on the floor.

2. Lay the two wooden sticks on the bag, 20 inches (50 cm) apart. Leave the same amount of bag on each side of the sticks.

3. Tape the sticks onto the bag. Make sure the ends of the sticks are firmly attached.

4. Cut two triangular side flaps from the bag, following the dotted lines on page 24.

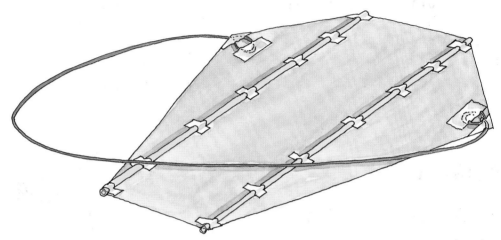

5. Cut a piece of string 13 feet (4 m) long and tie a loop at each end. This is the **bridle**. Tape the loops to the triangular side flaps. The loops should point toward the center of the kite.

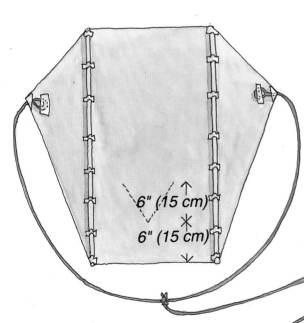

6" (15 cm)

6" (15 cm)

6. Make a small V-shaped cut in the kite, as shown. When the kite is flying, the cut will open to let air through. This helps the kite stay level.

7. Tie a long piece of string to the bridle string, and have a friend help you fly the kite.

KITE FLYING

Flying a kite

1. Let out about 11 feet (50 cm) of string.

2. Have a friend hold the kite high in the air. As soon as the kite catches the wind, let it fly on its own.

3. If the wind is strong, you can stand still and hold on to the string, letting out more string as the kite flies higher. If there is not much wind, you may need to run with your kite to make it fly.

WARNING:
Never fly a kite where there are electric cables or near a street or railroad tracks.

Further work

You can measure how strong the pull of your kite is. When it is flying in the air, attach the end of the string to the hook of a **spring balance**. Make sure you hold on tightly to the spring balance. Look to see where the marker is on the scale. Measure the pull on different days. Does it vary?

These kites have colorful pictures on them. What kind of decoration would you like to have on your kite? You could try painting some pictures of your own.

What You'll Need

More Books About Flight

Airplanes. David Peterson (Childrens Press)
Amazing Fact Book of Balloons. Marriott (Creative Education)
Catch the Wind! All about Kites. Gail Gibbons (Little, Brown)
Dirigibles. Joshua Stoff (Atheneum)
Finding Out about Things that Fly. K. Little and A. Thomas (EDC Publishing)
Flight and Floating. Alan Ward (EDC Publishing)
Helicopters. Norman S. Barrett (Franklin Watts)
Hovercraft. Angela Croome (Astor-Honor)
Leonardo Da Vinci: The Artist, Inventor, Scientist. Alice Provenson and Martin Provenson (Viking Kestrel)
The Mad Scientists' Club. Bertrand R. Brinley (Macrae Smith)
The Smithsonian Book of Flight for Young People. Walter J. Boyne (Macmillan)

More Books With Projects

Balloons: Building and Experimenting with Inflatable Toys. Bernie Zubrowski (Morrow)
Chinese Kites: How to Make and Fly Them. David F. Jue (C. E. Tuttle)
Easy to Make Spaceships That Really Fly. Mary Blockman and others (Prentice Hall)
The KnowHow Book of Flying Models: Lots of Models That Really Fly from Paper and Card. M. J. McNeil (EDC Publishing)
Paper Airplane Book. Seymour Smith (Puffin)
Paper Airplanes from Around the World. Ray Roberts (Aeronautic Instructional Resources)
Science Fun with Toy Boats and Planes. Rose Wyler (Simon and Schuster)

Places to Write for Science Supply Catalogs

White Wings
AG Industries, Inc.
3832 148th Avenue, NE
Redmond, Washington 98052

The Nature of Things
275 West Wisconsin Avenue
Milwaukee, Wisconsin 53203

Paul K. Guillow Inc.
40 New Salem Road
P. O. Box 229
Wakefield, Massachusetts 01880-0329

HMS Associates
2425 Maryland Road
Willow Grove, Pennsylvania 19090

 # GLOSSARY

bridle
A Y-shaped piece of rope used to hold and guide something.

design
To draw a plan for making something.

diameter
A straight line that passes through the center of a circle from a point on one side to a point on the other side.

gliders
Aircraft without engines that glide on currents of air.

hot-air balloons
Large bags filled with hot air or gas, able to lift passengers or equipment off the ground.

invention
The creation of a new machine.

jets
Airplanes powered by engines that produce a stream of hot gas to push the plane forward.

launch
To send an aircraft into the air or a boat into the water.

measure
To find out how big, long, or heavy something is or how quickly it moves.

passenger

A person who rides in a vehicle but does not help operate it.

rotor blades

The blades, or arms, of the propeller that spin around on top of a helicopter to lift it off the ground.

rudder

A flat, movable piece attached to the back of an airplane or boat, used for steering.

runway

A long, flat piece of level ground, used by airplanes for taking off and landing.

spring balance

A machine that measures how strong a pull is or how much something weighs. The hanging scales for produce in most supermarkets are spring balances.

Picture acknowledgements

The publishers would like to thank the following for allowing their photographs to be reproduced in this book: Heather Angel, p. 16; Cephas Picture Library, p. 12; Eye Ubiquitous, pp. 4, 27; Hutchison Library, pp. 15, 18; Topham Picture Library, p. 8; Timothy Woodcock, p. 20; Zefa, pp. 7, 11. Cover photography by Zul Mukhida.

INDEX